Chess Pedagogy for

Applicable Montessori Education

by

Dora Gomory

Bridges And Hearts Publishing

2024

All rights reserved.

Table of Content

Preface 3

Introduction 4

The Essence of Chess in Education 6

Chess and the Montessori Method..8

    Adapting Chess for Montessori and Developmental Stages 9

Cognitive and Academic Benefits of Chess 11

    Deepening Logical Thinking, Visualization, and Verbalization 11

    Chess in a Diverse Learning Environment 14

Social and Emotional Growth Through Chess 17

Implementing Chess in Education and Daily Life 19

Chess Pedagogy for Parents and Educators: Best Practices and Encouragement..23

Practical Chess Activities and Teaching Strategies 25

    Introducing the Chessboard: Montessori Principles on a Handmade Felt Board 25

    Learning the Letters A-H 29

    Learning Numbers and Number Concepts from 1 to 8 31

    Understanding and Learning Directions..37

    Introducing the Chess Pieces: "The Inhabitants of the Knight's Castle" Story....38

    Other Games to Prepare for Chess and Logical Thinking Development 41

Final Words..46

Preface

Imagine for a moment we're not talking about the grandmasters or the hallowed halls where silence reigns supreme over a chess match. Instead, let's think about a cozy living room on a lazy Sunday afternoon or a vibrant classroom where curiosity buzzes in the air. Here, chess isn't just a game; it's a secret doorway to a garden of untapped potential in the minds of our youngest learners.

Maria Montessori, a visionary who saw the extraordinary in the ordinary, once said, "The hands are the instruments of man's intelligence." It's through touching, moving, and engaging with the world that we truly learn. Chess, in this light, becomes more than a game. It's a tactile dance of decision and consequence, a playful yet profound tool in the developmental toolkit we offer our children.

This book is a conversation, a sharing of insights on how this ancient game becomes a contemporary teacher. It's for parents who dream of more for their children and educators who strive to bring those dreams to life. Together, we'll explore how chess can sharpen minds, enrich hearts, and through several practical examples we can weave a little more wonder into the fabric of education.

Introduction

Why chess, you might ask? Well, it's a bit like life itself, isn't it? A board set with pieces that move in unique ways, facing challenges, making decisions, and living with the outcomes, whether they lead to triumph or teach a hard-learned lesson. At its core, chess mirrors the strategic, sometimes whimsical, often challenging game we all play every day.

From an early age, children should be guided towards independence and taught to gradually assume responsibility for their actions and work. When a child makes a sudden decision—like hitting someone, taking a toy, or knocking over a glass—they must face the consequences, such as cleaning up spilled water, apologizing, or returning the toy.

What sets chess apart from other activities, including many sports, is its unique blend of art, science, and sport. While it may not build physical strength, it rigorously trains the mind, shaping how a player approaches life. The skills and qualities developed through chess—critical thinking, foresight, and responsibility—are invaluable in today's world.

To cultivate these traits, it's important to spark a child's interest in chess from a young age, inviting them into this mysterious and fascinating world. Children are open to anything and absorb everything, as long as it's presented to them in the right way. Their minds are like sponges, capable of soaking up all they encounter without ever overflowing.

While they may only recognize patterns and connections later, during their early school years, they are constantly storing information, ready to retrieve and apply it when needed. What a child learns through experience during this formative period becomes a fundamental part of them, something they never forget.

Even at a young age, we begin preparing them for "evaluating positions," making decisions, and solving life's challenges quickly, decisively, and fairly.

Think of this book as your go-to guide—a sort of map through the enchanting world of chess as more than a pastime—a tool, a teacher, a treasure trove of lessons waiting to be discovered. It's a journey into how the game can fine-tune the mind, warm the heart, and maybe even shape a soul or two along the way.

We'll wander through the history, sneak a peek into classrooms where chess becomes a language of learning, and sit down with families where game night turns into a masterclass in life skills. From the steadfast principles of Montessori to the bustling energy of a modern classroom, we'll see how chess can be the thread that ties it all together.

Shall we begin? Let's explore, question, and maybe even redefine what it means to learn, teach, and grow. After all, in the game of chess, like in life, every move counts, every decision shapes us, and every game leaves us a little wiser, ready for the next challenge.

The Essence of Chess in Education

A Game of Infinite Learning

When we think of chess, images of intense concentration, strategic moves, and perhaps even historic matches may come to mind. Yet, beyond the checkered board lies a realm ripe with educational potential, particularly for the nimble minds of young learners.

Chess, often referred to as the "game of kings," has traversed through centuries, evolving not just as a pastime but as a tool for mental and moral development. But can our own children become kings these days? And how?

The Intellectual Ballet

Consider for a moment the chessboard as a stage, each piece performing in an intellectual ballet. The pawns, knights, bishops, and others don't merely move; they tell stories of strategy, sacrifice, and foresight. It's here, in these stories, that children find a playground for their developing minds, learning to anticipate consequences, think critically, and navigate the complex interplay of multiple decisions.

In this ballet of minds, every child holds the potential to command the stage, to be the maestro of their own game. But what does it take for them to realize this potential?

Chess and Historical Insight

Historically, chess has been a mirror reflecting the strategic thinking of its era. By integrating chess into education, we offer children a glimpse into the past, connecting them with the thought leaders and strategists of ancient and medieval times. This historical perspective enriches their understanding of chess as a game deeply woven into the human experience, fostering a deeper appreciation for history and culture.

Can the echoes of these ancient games stir a sense of wisdom and strategy in the hearts of our young learners? How do we bridge centuries of knowledge into today's lesson plans?

A Modern Educational Tool

In today's classrooms, chess serves as a dynamic educational tool, bridging the gap between learning and play. It's here that abstract concepts like planning, analysis, and problem-solving come to life. Each game of chess is a new puzzle to solve, a challenge that prompts students to apply logic, patience, and creativity.

The question then arises: in our fast-paced, digital world, how can the slow, thoughtful game of chess capture the imagination of our young ones? How do we make the ancient art of strategy appealing to the TikTok generation?

Embracing Chess in Education

As we weave chess into the fabric of education, we're not just teaching children to play a game. We're inviting them into a rich tradition of learning, thinking, and growing. We're giving them tools—not just to win on the board but to navigate the myriad challenges and opportunities life presents.

In this journey, the real challenge lies not in teaching chess, but in instilling a love for the game and its lessons. How do we ensure that this ancient game does not become just another subject to study but a beloved companion in the journey of learning?

Incorporating chess into educational settings isn't merely about cultivating future chess champions; it's about enriching young minds. It's about offering them a form of play that challenges, inspires, and teaches all at once. Through chess, children learn to see several moves ahead, not just on the board, but in life, equipping them with the foresight and resilience needed for the future.

As we lay down the chessboard, we're not just setting up a game; we're setting the stage for a lifetime of learning. But the question remains: how do we move beyond the game, to instill the lessons of chess into the very fabric of our children's lives?

Chess and the Montessori Method

The Montessori Method, celebrated for its focus on self-directed activity, hands-on learning, and collaborative play, offers a natural alliance with the game of chess. This alliance not only enriches the educational landscape but also nurtures a child's development in a uniquely holistic way.

Aligning Chess with Montessori Principles

Chess mirrors the Montessori ethos of fostering independence through exploration. The game invites learners to engage with complex concepts in an accessible, tactile manner.

When pondering how our children can navigate their own kingdoms, the Montessori chessboard emerges as a realm of infinite possibilities. Here, each learner, regardless of their role—be it king or pawn—discovers the significance of strategic thinking.

The Role of the Educator

In the Montessori classroom, the educator's role as a guide is paramount. This role becomes even more nuanced when integrating chess, where the emphasis shifts to inspiring curiosity rather than imparting knowledge directly.

Facilitating rather than instructing, we allow children to explore chess at their own pace, discovering its joys and challenges through personal experience. How, then, do we balance guidance with freedom? The key lies in creating an environment where the chess pieces themselves invite inquiry and exploration.

Chess as a Hands-on Learning Tool

Chess transforms into a powerful hands-on learning experience under the Montessori method. Each piece's movement, each game's unfolding narrative, becomes a lesson in decision-making, critical thinking, and creative problem-solving.

The silent question lingers: will the introspective nature of chess truly engage the dynamic minds of young learners? Montessori answers with a strategy of empowerment, turning the chessboard into a canvas for imagination and exploration.

Deepening the Integration

Rather than carving out exclusive periods for chess instruction, we weave chess-related activities into the fabric of daily learning, aligning with Montessori's holistic approach. This integration fosters an environment where children naturally encounter and engage with chess, learning its lessons as part of their broader educational journey.

This approach addresses the challenge of making chess a living, breathing part of children's learning landscape. How do we ensure that chess is seen not merely as a subject to be mastered but as a fascinating world to be explored? By embedding chess within the Montessori framework, we make every piece, every move, a discovery waiting to happen.

As we continue to intertwine chess with the Montessori Method, we're not just teaching a game; we're inviting children into a dialogue with history, strategy, and themselves. This dialogue opens doors to new ways of thinking, problem-solving, and learning, offering lessons that resonate far beyond the confines of the chessboard.

Adapting Chess for Montessori and Developmental Stages

In the Montessori approach, activities are tailored to the developmental needs and interests of the child, encouraging exploration, discovery, and learning through hands-on experience. Chess, with its rich potential for fostering critical thinking, concentration, and problem-solving skills, is no exception. However, the traditional game of chess, as seen in parks and world championships, can be complex and intimidating for young learners. This necessitates a thoughtful adaptation of the game to make it accessible, engaging, and educationally fruitful for children.

To bridge this gap, Montessori educators often introduce simplified versions of chess. These adaptations maintain the essence of the game while making it approachable for young minds. For example:

- **Mini-Games Focused on Individual Pieces**: Before diving into full games, children might first explore mini-games that focus on understanding the movement and role of individual chess pieces. This step-by-step approach helps build a solid foundation of the game's rules and strategies in a manageable way.
- **Chess Puzzles and Scenarios**: Instead of playing full games, children might work on specific chess puzzles or scenarios. These activities can highlight particular strategies or concepts, allowing children to practice problem-solving and critical thinking skills in a focused manner.
- **Storytelling with Chess**: Incorporating storytelling into chess activities can transform the learning experience. By assigning characters and narratives to the pieces, children engage with the game on a creative and imaginative level, making the abstract rules of chess more tangible and memorable.

The purpose of adapting chess in a Montessori setting is distinct from that of competitive play. While traditional chess aims to cultivate skills for competition, the Montessori adaptations of chess emphasize:

- **Cognitive Development**: Simplified chess games are designed to enhance cognitive abilities such as memory, concentration, and logical reasoning.
- **Social-Emotional Growth**: Through collaborative play and problem-solving, children learn about sportsmanship, empathy, patience, and dealing with both success and setbacks.
- **Cross-Curricular Connections**: Chess is used as a tool to connect with other areas of learning, from math and geometry (understanding grids and spatial awareness) to history and art (exploring the history of chess and designing chess pieces).

In later sections, we will provide detailed examples of how these simplified chess games and purpose-driven adaptations are implemented in Montessori classrooms. Educators and parents will gain insights into practical ways to introduce chess concepts, tailor activities to different age groups, and integrate chess into the broader educational experience.

Cognitive and Academic Benefits of Chess

Chess is not merely a game of strategic conquests and intellectual duels; it's a powerful educational tool that sharpens the mind and enriches academic learning. As we venture into the cognitive and academic benefits of chess, let's consider how this ancient game can be a modern boon to childhood education.

Enhancing Cognitive Skills

Chess, with its intricate strategies and endless possibilities, is like a gym for the mind. But how exactly does pushing wooden pieces across a board make us smarter?

Research and observation have shown that engaging with chess leads to improved problem-solving skills, heightened concentration, and enhanced memory. Each move on the chessboard requires a player to think critically, anticipate their opponent's actions, and consider the consequences of their own decisions.

For young learners, this isn't just about outsmarting an opponent; it's about building a framework for analytical thinking that applies both in and out of the classroom.

Deepening Logical Thinking, Visualization, and Verbalization

Chess enhances the development of logical thinking, visualization, and verbalization in the following areas:

- **Spatial Awareness**: Recognizing and understanding positions on the board. Children learn to perceive the board as a whole and identify the relative positions of pieces.
- **Essence Recognition**: Identifying what is important and which pieces to maneuver. This helps children focus on the most critical aspects of any given situation.

- **Problem Sensitivity:** Detecting potential issues on the board, which fosters an ability to foresee and address challenges.
- **Algorithmic Thinking:** Anticipating the correct sequence of moves by recalling past experiences and learned strategies. This skill translates directly to real-life problem-solving.
- **Differentiated Abstraction:** Drawing conclusions based on previous experiences, allowing for more sophisticated decision-making.
- **Analogy:** Developing winning positions by drawing parallels from past games or situations, a skill that enhances strategic thinking.
- **Combinatorial Thinking:** Mentally projecting various potential moves and their outcomes, fostering the ability to consider multiple possibilities simultaneously.
- **Comparison:** Identifying similarities and differences between the game and possible moves, enhancing analytical skills.

Cross-Curricular Connections

Chess is often siloed as an extracurricular activity, but what if we viewed it as a cross-curricular bridge, connecting dots across diverse subjects?

By integrating chess into the curriculum, educators can create rich, interdisciplinary learning experiences. For example, the history of chess can complement lessons in world history, while the design of chess pieces can inspire art projects. These connections not only make learning more engaging but also help students see the relevance of their studies in a broader context.

Examples of Practical Applications

To make these cognitive benefits more tangible, let's explore some practical applications that can be incorporated into educational settings:

- **Spatial Perception Exercises:** Children can use their bodies to simulate the movement of chess pieces on a large, painted chessboard. This helps them understand how each piece moves (e.g., right-left, forward-backward) while also reinforcing concepts like counting squares.
- **Speed Development Games:** Two children, representing opposing pieces (e.g., light and dark), follow instructions to move as pawns. They start by moving two squares forward and then practice

competing to see who can move faster—without stakes, to ensure that everyone is praised for their effort.
- **Shadow Play**: One child mirrors another's every move, acting as their "shadow." This game reinforces the concept of mirroring an opponent's strategy, an essential skill in chess.
- **Decision-Making Drills**: Children practice making quick decisions based on which piece they represent and how it should move (e.g., direction and number of squares). This helps them develop both decision-making speed and accuracy.

Boosting Academic Performance

The leap from the chessboard to academic achievement might seem a long one. Yet, could the focus and foresight developed in chess translate to better grades and classroom behavior?

Studies suggest a strong correlation between regular chess play and academic performance, particularly in mathematics and reading comprehension. Chess requires the decoding of complex patterns and the understanding of rules, skills directly applicable to mathematical reasoning and linguistic fluency.

Imagine a classroom where lessons in geometry are intertwined with chess strategies, where narrative skills are honed through the stories of legendary games and players.

Cross-Curricular Connections

Chess is often siloed as an extracurricular activity, but what if we viewed it as a cross-curricular bridge, connecting dots across diverse subjects?

By integrating chess into the curriculum, educators can create rich, interdisciplinary learning experiences. For example, the history of chess can complement lessons in world history, while the design of chess pieces can inspire art projects.

How then, do we ensure that chess is seen not just as a game, but as a versatile educational tool? The answer lies in creativity and integration, making chess a thread that weaves through the fabric of our educational tapestries.

Personal Reflections and Classroom Stories

Incorporating personal anecdotes and classroom stories can illustrate the transformative impact of chess on individual learners. Whether it's the quiet student who found their voice through chess club or the struggling mathematician who learned to love numbers through the game, these stories are a testament to chess's power to change lives.

Reflecting on my own journey with chess, I'm reminded of the lessons of patience, perseverance, and humility it taught me. Chess, in its essence, is a dialogue between players, between past and present, between the game and life itself.

Chess in a Diverse Learning Environment

Mr. Thompson, an elementary school teacher with a passion for chess, observed that his class of 20 students, each with their unique learning styles and challenges, often struggled to engage with traditional teaching methods. Inspired to make a difference, he decided to introduce chess as a tool for learning and engagement. His goal wasn't just to teach them how to play chess but to use the game as a medium to enhance their cognitive skills, self-esteem, and social interactions.

To accommodate the varied learning needs of his students, Mr. Thompson designed a tiered chess program. He started with the basics of chess, using large, tactile chess pieces that helped students with fine motor skill challenges. For those who found the rules overwhelming, he introduced simplified chess games, focusing on one piece at a time, such as "The Knight's Tour," where students would only learn how the knight moves and try to visit every square on the board without repeating a square.

Among Mr. Thompson's students was Jamie, a child diagnosed with dyslexia, who often felt frustrated and disengaged during reading and writing activities. Chess became a transformative tool for Jamie. The visual and spatial aspects of the game, such as planning the movement of pieces and visualizing the board, played to Jamie's strengths. Chess also provided a non-verbal medium for Jamie to demonstrate strategic thinking and problem-solving skills, areas where Jamie excelled but had few opportunities to showcase in traditional academic settings.

Over the course of the school year, Mr. Thompson noticed remarkable changes in Jamie and other students. Jamie, who previously hesitated to participate in class discussions, now eagerly engaged in chess-based problem-solving activities, showing a newfound confidence. Moreover, chess facilitated peer interactions, encouraging students to communicate, collaborate, and even mentor each other on strategies, fostering a supportive classroom community.

Mr. Thompson reflected on the experience, noting, "Chess provided a unique avenue for students like Jamie to shine, revealing abilities that our standard curriculum had overlooked. It's not just about the game; it's about recognizing and nurturing each child's potential, building their confidence, and helping them connect with their peers. Chess became more than a learning tool; it was a catalyst for transformation in our classroom."

Ms. Rodriguez, a bilingual education teacher, introduced chess to her English language learners (ELL) to support language development and cultural integration. Recognizing the universal appeal of chess, she used it as a common ground for students from diverse linguistic backgrounds.

Chess was incorporated into language lessons as a way to introduce new vocabulary and encourage conversational practice. Ms. Rodriguez created a "chess word of the day" activity, where students learned chess-related terms in both English and their native languages, promoting not only language acquisition but also cross-cultural understanding.

Carlos, a recent immigrant with limited English proficiency, found chess to be a gateway to improving his language skills. Through the game, he learned new words and phrases, which he practiced with peers during chess activities. This interactive, engaging approach to language learning helped Carlos become more confident in his English communication skills.

Ms. Rodriguez observed that chess facilitated a supportive learning environment where students felt comfortable practicing their new language skills in a real-world context. The shared interest in chess led to increased student interaction, peer tutoring, and a sense of community among ELL students.

Reflecting on the success of integrating chess into her language lessons, Ms. Rodriguez noted, "Chess became more than just a teaching tool; it was a bridge connecting our students' diverse cultures and languages. It fostered a classroom culture of mutual respect, curiosity, and a shared love for learning."

Social and Emotional Growth Through Chess

Chess is often celebrated for its intellectual benefits, but its role in fostering social and emotional growth is equally profound. Beyond the cognitive leaps it encourages, chess serves as a mirror reflecting the emotional and social dynamics of life itself. This chapter explores how the ancient game of chess cultivates empathy, resilience, self-awareness, and the ability to navigate social interactions with grace and strategy.

Chess teaches players to see the board from their opponent's perspective, a skill that translates into real-world empathy. Understanding an opponent's strategy in chess mirrors the ability to understand another person's thoughts and feelings in life.

How often do we truly try to see the world from someone else's vantage point? Chess offers a structured way to practice this skill, reinforcing the importance of empathy in our everyday interactions.

Resilience is forged in the moments after a loss, in choosing to see defeat not as a setback but as a learning opportunity. Chess provides a safe space for young learners to experience loss, analyze their missteps, and develop a healthier relationship with failure.

Remembering the first time I lost a game of chess, I felt devastated. Yet, it was through that loss that I learned the most valuable lessons about perseverance and the courage to try again.

Chess demands a level of self-awareness and emotional control rare in other competitive activities. Players learn to manage their emotions, from the thrill of a well-executed strategy to the frustration of an unforeseen defeat, cultivating a balanced emotional state.

Reflective Pause: Chess, in its quiet intensity, teaches us that our greatest adversary is often our own impulsive reactions. How can mastering emotional regulation in chess help us navigate life's more turbulent moments?

Though chess is a game between two individuals, it fosters a sense of community and teamwork, especially in club and tournament settings.

Players learn to communicate effectively, share strategies, and support one another, reinforcing the value of social bonds and collaborative effort.

The chess club was more than a place to play; it was where I found a sense of belonging and camaraderie. How do these experiences shape our understanding of community and cooperation?

In a diverse middle school, the chess club became an unexpected venue for fostering empathy among students. Sarah, a skilled player, was initially competitive and focused solely on her advancement. However, the club's mentor encouraged her to teach beginners, pairing her with Alex, a newcomer with a keen interest but little experience.

Through teaching Alex, Sarah began to see the game from a beginner's perspective, recognizing the challenges and frustrations she had once overcome. This role reversal from competitor to mentor not only improved Sarah's empathy towards less experienced players but also enriched her understanding of the game.

In their journey, the quiet moments spent pondering moves became opportunities for sharing life experiences, bridging gaps between very different individuals and fostering a deep sense of empathy and understanding.

Mark, a high school student, faced a tough loss in a regional chess tournament. Initially disheartened, he contemplated giving up the game he loved. His coach, recognizing the teachable moment, sat down with him to review the game, focusing not on the loss but on the learning opportunities it presented.

Reflecting on this experience, Mark realized that each move, whether leading to victory or defeat, was a step towards becoming a better player. This mindset shift, from viewing loss as failure to seeing it as a growth opportunity, was pivotal in building his resilience, not just in chess but in facing life's challenges.

A classroom implementation of chess as a behavioral management tool showed surprising results in enhancing students' self-awareness and emotional regulation. Jenny, known for her impulsive behavior, struggled to focus and often acted out in frustration during class activities.

Introducing chess into the daily routine, the teacher used the game's requirement for patience and strategic thinking as a mirror for self-reflection. Jenny, drawn to the game's quiet intensity, began to notice her impulses and, over time, learned to pause and think before acting, both on the board and in the classroom.

A community center's chess club, open to all ages, became a melting pot of social interaction and teamwork. Here, retirees shared tables with teenagers, exchanging not only chess strategies but also life lessons. The club organized team-based tournaments, requiring players to collaborate and communicate effectively, reinforcing the importance of teamwork.

Elder member George and teenager Liam formed an unlikely but successful team, their combined experience and youthful energy proving complementary. Through their partnership, members observed firsthand the power of diverse perspectives and the value of cooperation.

Implementing Chess in Education and Daily Life

Embracing Chess at Home and School

The journey of introducing chess into our lives isn't just about learning to move pieces on a board; it's about opening a gateway to a world rich with strategic thought, patience, and countless life lessons. Whether at the kitchen table or in the classroom, chess offers a unique blend of entertainment and education, a tool that sharpens minds and forges connections.

But don't you worry, there are ways and places to find resources even on a busy day. From online tutorials that simplify complex strategies to community chess clubs that welcome players of all ages, the world of chess is more accessible than ever before.

Tailoring Chess Education to Individual Needs

Chess, in its essence, is a dialogue—between players, between moves, and between the myriad strategies that unfold with each game. This dialogue is as diverse as the children and students we aim to teach. Some may find joy in the silent tension of thought before a move; others may revel in the stories that each piece can tell.

But how do we cater to such a wide array of interests and abilities?

Flexibility is our greatest ally here. For the younger ones, chess can be a story, a battle between kingdoms, where learning the game comes through tales of heroism and adventure. For others, it might be the challenge, the competition, or the sheer joy of learning something new that draws them in.

Starting a Chess Program: Practical Steps

Launching a chess program or club can seem daunting at first glance.

Where do I even begin?

Start simple. A few boards, some eager players, and a space to gather are all you really need to get the ball rolling. The internet is a treasure trove of free resources, from instructional videos to printable chess puzzles, making it easier than ever to kickstart your chess journey.

Remember, the heart of a successful chess program lies not in grand tournaments or pristine boards but in the community it builds and the curiosity it ignites.

But what if we have limited resources?

Creativity becomes your resource. Use homemade pieces, draw boards on cardboard, and see each limitation as an opportunity to innovate.

Cross-Curricular Chess: Enhancing Academic and Life Skills

Chess is a chameleon, capable of blending into the fabric of nearly any academic subject.

But can a game really enhance academic learning?

Absolutely. In math, chess teaches strategy and foresight. In history, it offers a window into the past, and in art, it inspires creativity through the design of pieces and boards.

Imagine integrating chess into a history lesson, exploring the game's evolution over centuries, or using chess strategies to solve mathematical problems. The key is to view chess not just as a game, but as a versatile educational tool that complements and enhances learning across disciplines.

Encouraging Personal Growth Through Chess

At its core, chess is a journey of personal growth, a path that challenges us to think deeply, act strategically, and feel passionately. It teaches resilience in the face of defeat, humility in victory, and the value of patience and hard work.

But isn't chess just for those with a competitive streak?

On the contrary, chess offers a space for every child to explore, learn, and grow, regardless of their competitive nature. It's a tool for teaching life's most valuable lessons, wrapped in the guise of a game.

> The Johnsons decided to introduce chess to their family routine, dedicating Thursday nights to the game. Initially, it was about learning the rules and the joy of playing together. **"But we discovered something deeper,"** Mrs. Johnson reflects. The nights became a forum for discussing strategies, which spilled over into conversations about making thoughtful decisions in life and considering the consequences of actions.

> Ms. Patel introduced chess into her culturally diverse classroom as a universal language that all her students could understand and appreciate. She noticed how students who struggled with traditional subjects found confidence on the chessboard. **"Chess became a way for them to express themselves, to shine in ways they hadn't before,"** she notes. It wasn't long before chess discussions became a catalyst for deeper connections among students, breaking down barriers and fostering a sense of belonging and mutual respect.

Chess Pedagogy for Parents and Educators: Best Practices and Encouragement

Do you remember when we asked in the beginning what makes chess more than just a game?

It's its unparalleled capacity to foster cognitive, emotional, and social growth in children. Chess pedagogy isn't just about teaching a child to move pieces; it's about opening a world of strategic thinking, patience, and problem-solving.

Introducing chess at home should be an adventure, filled with discovery and laughter.

Have you ever watched a child's eyes light up when they learn a new concept or win a game they thought was lost?

That joy is what we're aiming for. You shouldn't stress out about making every session a lesson. Instead, focus on the shared experience, whether it's a dramatic retelling of historical chess matches or creating your own chess stories.

For educators looking to weave chess into the fabric of their curriculum, remember, inclusivity is key.

Have you ever considered the silent observer in the classroom, the child who hesitates to participate?

Chess can be a bridge, connecting academic concepts with real-world applications and providing a platform for every student to engage and shine. From math puzzles that mimic chess strategies to history lessons on famous chess matches, the opportunities are endless.

Every child brings their own set of skills to the chessboard, just as they do to life.

Do you remember the emphasis on recognizing and nurturing each child's unique journey with chess?

Some may excel in the quiet strategy of the game, while others find joy in the social interactions it encourages. There's no one right way to learn or teach chess, so be flexible and attentive to what works best for each student or child.

Best practices in chess education revolve around balance - between learning and play, challenge and support, competition and collaboration.

You shouldn't stress out over ensuring that every game is a lesson.

Instead, view each session as an opportunity to foster growth, curiosity, and a love for the game. Encourage students and children to reflect on their games, consider alternative strategies, and most importantly, learn from every move.

Remember, you're not alone. The chess community is vast and supportive, with countless resources available for those willing to seek them out. From online forums and tutorials to local chess clubs and tournaments, the opportunities for learning and connection are boundless.

Chess pedagogy is a path we walk alongside our students and children, filled with discovery, challenges, and achievements.

Have you ever pondered the true victory in chess? I

t's not the checkmate, but the journey there—the lessons learned, the skills honed, and the joy shared. Chess is a companion in life's adventure, a teacher of invaluable lessons that extend well beyond the game.

Practical Chess Activities and Teaching Strategies

Introducing the Chessboard: Montessori Principles on a Handmade Felt Board

Children are encouraged to freely explore and interact with the chessboard and pieces. Initially, the 8x8 grid and the alternating black and white squares may seem overwhelming to young minds. To ease this, I created a smaller felt board with a 2x2 grid, then expanded to a 4x4 grid, where children can correctly place black squares, effectively breaking down the 8x8 unit into more manageable parts. This approach offers multiple variations for children to experiment with. They begin by placing black squares on the 2x2 and 4x4 boards, ensuring that the lower-left corner always contains a black square. Once they've mastered this task, which they experience as a fascinating game, they progress to placing four 4x4 boards on a larger 8x8 felt board, positioning the black squares accordingly.

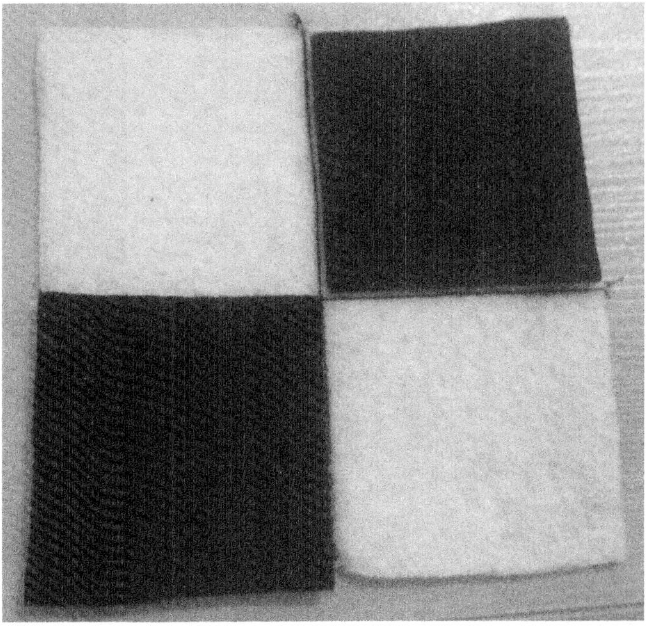

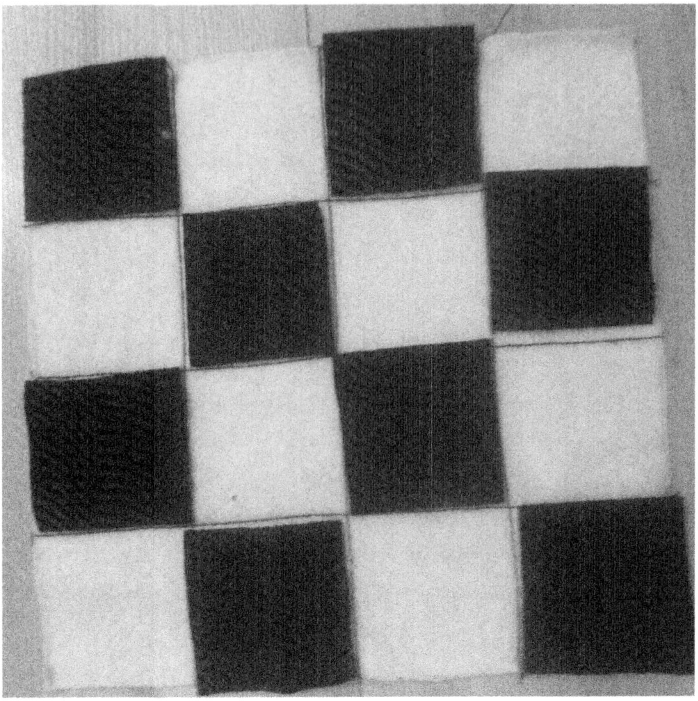

A fundamental aspect of Montessori tools is self-correction, which I've incorporated here. I laminated cards of appropriate size, each featuring a small figure in the center to indicate the child's position. The large white rectangle on the right shows the correct alignment (side position). Small white or black dots are placed on the squares. When the child places the card on the felt board, they should see squares matching the color of the dots. If the colors match, the task is correct. If not, the child can correct their mistake, repeating the process as often as needed until they consistently achieve the correct solution. Following this, the child places the black squares on an 8x8 white felt board, now using a smaller reference board, requiring them to scale down the proportions visually.

Next, we observe the large outdoor chessboard, discussing how it's composed of white and black squares. Children are invited to explore the board, moving freely and even hopping from square to square—on one leg, two legs, or following different patterns. We noticed that many children preferred stepping or jumping only on white or only on black squares. As they grew more comfortable, they began moving not just forward but also sideways, right and left, and eventually, even backwards.

The children can also play tag on the board. In the classroom, the chessboard is always set up on the chess table, accessible for the children to play with at any time. "Montessori children" enjoy arranging and categorizing objects based on their own ideas and experiences—whether by color, size, shape, or other criteria. They will undoubtedly do the same with the chess pieces.

Learning the Letters A-H

A: apple, ant
B: bear, bird
C: cat, car
D: duck, dinosaur
E: elephant, egg
F: frog, flower
G: goat, grape
H: hat, horse

Young children are often unfamiliar with letters, so it's essential to introduce them to the letters used in chess, from A to H. We gather words that start with each of these eight letters, using objects placed in a basket to make the learning process engaging and varied. The children are encouraged to connect the sounds with the objects they find most appealing. Outside, we practice on the large painted chessboard by placing a large wooden "C" in front of the child. The caregiver pronounces the letter "C," and the child identifies objects from the basket that contain the "C" sound. Over time, they will be able to identify the letter "C" in the middle or at the end of words as well.

As children successfully match objects with the corresponding letters, they begin searching for words that start with those letters in books and around the room. The child selects their favorite objects and associates them with the letters placed beside the chessboard. In the next stage, the child independently places the letters and objects, eventually only pairing the letters with the appropriate squares. This requires extended practice.

Simultaneously, children also engage in activities to develop their gross motor skills. For example, we write the letters on the pavement with chalk, and the children walk or jump over them. The movement can be paired with verbalization, where the child says the name of an object or the sound associated with the letter as they move. They also enjoy fine motor activities, such as tracing letters with their fingers, molding them from clay, cutting them out, or drawing them in a tray filled with flour or sand. A particularly fun activity is when one or two children use their bodies to form the shape of a letter.

Learning Numbers and Number Concepts from 1 to 8

As with letters, the goal here is to familiarize children with the concept of numbers before introducing the digits themselves. We teach the numbers and associated concepts from 1 to 8.
Children count by clapping their hands or stepping while counting. They practice counting while moving across the chessboard, reinforcing the concept that they move "from the bottom up," that is, vertically.

Children place pebbles on specific squares and count them. To connect counting with movement, we introduce the following exercise: the number of steps a child takes corresponds to the number of objects they are given, such as pebbles or blocks. They may be instructed to only step on white or black squares, adding directional commands like "step forward two white squares" or "step one black square to the right."

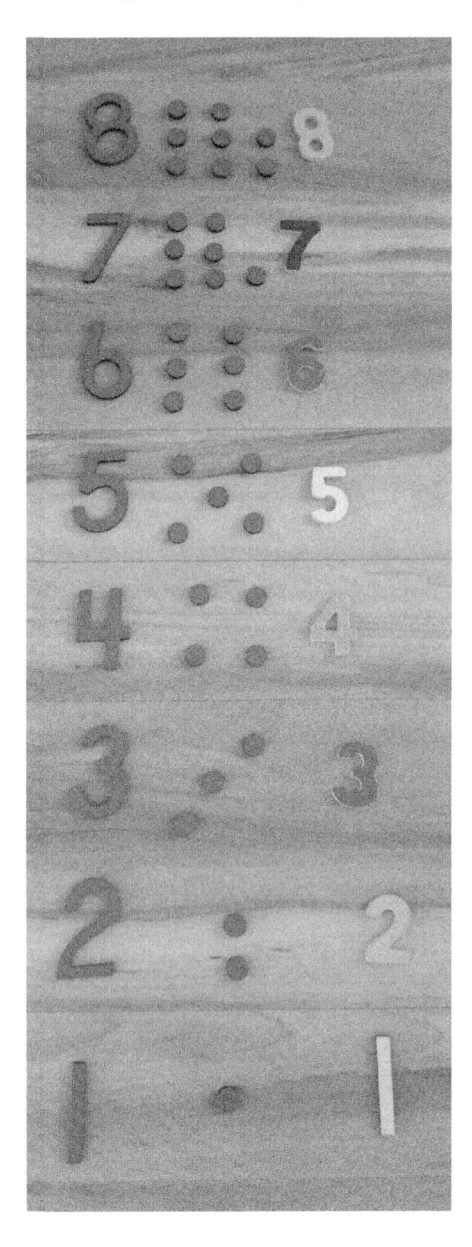

The first step in teaching numbers is to associate one object with another. For instance, a bear is paired with a plate, a small spoon, and a fork. We always count the items, explaining that the bear has one plate, one spoon, and one fork. For two cats, we place food in two small bowls, and for three dogs, we assign three leashes, and so on. The children also place counters and large wooden numerals next to these objects.

Once the child can count to eight, we place counters beside the chessboard, numbered from 1 to 8. Simultaneously, they practice associating the counters and other objects with the corresponding numerals using Montessori materials. This helps them grasp the concept of numbers connected to quantity. Both indoors and outdoors, they practice by taking steps: for example, "three steps," meaning they step on three squares.

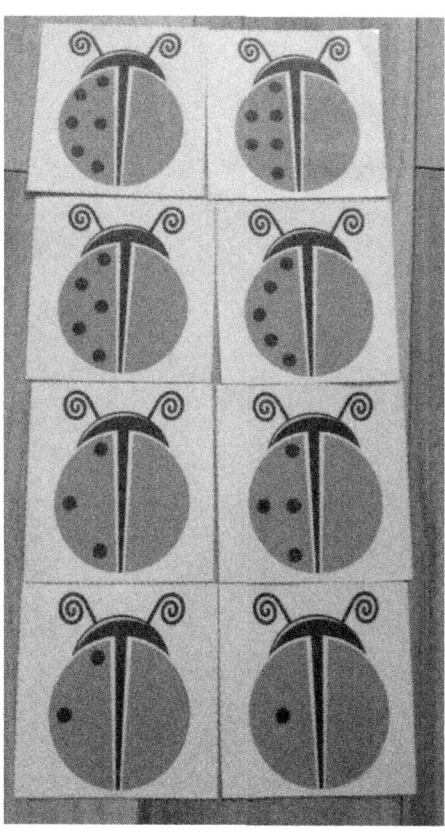

As a supplementary activity, to reinforce the concept of grouping, children play tag, dividing into white and black teams. Those caught must squat down, and the winning team is the one with the most players left standing.

Understanding and Learning Directions

Spatial orientation is a crucial aspect of school readiness, making it important for children to learn the concepts of right and left.
We tie a red ribbon on the children's right wrists to reinforce the right side. We use gloves from the Montessori set: the child places their left hand in the left glove, the right hand in the right glove (the right glove has a red pom-pom). We verbally reinforce these concepts at all times.

Physical exercises are used to practice and reinforce right and left sides. For example, "raise your right hand, then your left hand," "take a step to the right, then a step to the left." As they walk in a circle, they stop, take one step to the right, and one step to the left. In the game of Simon Says, children are instructed to "touch your left ear with your right hand," or "hold the teddy bear in your left hand." They may also throw a ball with their right hand, then with their left. Walking with the right foot on a bench and the left on the ground helps develop body schema and coordination.

Children also practice moving forward, backward, and diagonally through guided exercises. With their eyes closed, a partner directs them forward, backward, and then combines these directions with right, left, and diagonal movements.

Nursery Rhyme:
"One, two, buckle my shoe.
Three, four, shut the door.
Five, six, pick up sticks.
Seven, eight, lay them straight."

In this exercise, the adult stands with their back to the children, so they don't confuse directions. Once the children are confident in recognizing directions, the adult faces them to give instructions, creating a situation similar to chess, where the opponent mirrors the child's moves. This prepares them for reversed thinking.

Statue Game:
Children take turns standing with their backs to the others, assuming different poses or performing activities for the others to imitate. They also name the movements, encouraging motivation and development.

Introducing the Chess Pieces: "The Inhabitants of the Knight's Castle" Story

We introduce the chess pieces, naming them as the children hold them, reinforcing the tactile memory of each piece. We discuss what each piece resembles or reminds them of.
Simultaneously, children can see and touch a variety of chess pieces in both two and three dimensions. They are free to arrange and group these pieces according to criteria they come up with themselves.

For each piece, we tell a story. We also place symbols of the chess pieces on the appropriate parts of the climbing structure. After hearing each story, the children climb to the corresponding spot on the outdoor play equipment, representing the hierarchical position of the chess pieces. Children are assigned specific roles, and their positions on the equipment represent the hierarchy of the chess pieces. They use simple symbols to identify their roles (e.g., a crown for the king or queen, a shield and sword for the rook, a letter for the bishop, a horse symbol for the knight, and no symbol for the pawn). The vertical height helps them understand the hierarchy: the king stands at the top, followed by the queen, the rooks, the bishops, and the knights, with the pawns at the bottom. The children take their positions as they listen to the story.

Throughout the activity, the adult repeats the names of the pieces, and the children also repeat them, gradually learning the names of all the pieces. This process can be repeated by retelling the story as often as needed. After becoming familiar with the pieces, the children arrange them according to criteria set by the educator. For instance, they may pair white and black pieces, or match each piece with its corresponding color. They might also pair pieces by size, material, or value. It's an intriguing task for them to compare and pair three-dimensional pieces with their two-dimensional counterparts, or even with their own drawings. Consistent repetition of the names of the pieces is required.

For older children with more developed fine motor skills, worksheets can be created with various developmental goals in mind.
To enhance tactile perception, pieces can be placed in a mystery bag, where children try to identify them by touch alone.

After role-playing multiple times and learning about hierarchy, the children draw or build a knight's castle using small boxes or building blocks, placing the pieces (either three-dimensional or two-dimensional) in the correct positions.

In this task, children must place the appropriate number of pieces from the actual chessboard onto the knight's castle they've built.
This leads to a new task: inventory management. They count how many pawns, knights, bishops, rooks, queens, and kings are present in both the white and black pieces, then match the corresponding numbers. (Younger children can place an equal number of counters, nuts, etc., for each piece.) They compare which piece has more or less and create a sequence from the most to the least, then reverse the order.

Recognizing Pieces in Two Dimensions:
Children trace the pieces, color them in, and cut them out, creating the same number of pieces as would be placed on a board. (They create both white and black teams.) Differentiated worksheets are designed for various levels within this theme, taking into account the children's age and internal developmental progress.

Chess Piece Puzzle:
Children assemble cut-out pieces of chess pieces into a puzzle. (We create puzzles with 3, 4, 5, or 6 pieces, also differentiated based on the child's ability.)
Under extraordinary circumstances, castles are also built from snow, with one castle flying a white flag and the other a black flag. In this task, the inhabitants of the two castles become opponents and engage in battle (in the form of a snowball fight or a soft ball battle). Although the goal in chess is victory, this also teaches children to cope with failure.

Preparation for Position Evaluation:
Objective: To improve short-term memory, recall, and speed by remembering the position and movement of multiple objects.

Memory cards featuring chess pieces are used; children arrange them and reveal the pairs.
Children place 3, 4, 5, or more plush animals or toys on a table, observe them briefly, and then cover them. Their task is to recall and show which animals or toys are hidden under the cloth.

Variations:

- Turning away makes it more challenging to recall the covered animals.
- One or more animals on the table change position; the child must identify which one moved and from where.
- This game can also be played with cards in two dimensions.
- Standing in a circle outdoors, children make eye contact and switch places, or two children exchange places upon hearing their names called (they must remember where each stood). The game becomes more challenging when played with a parachute, as the children cannot always see their partner and must rely more on their memory.

Other Games to Prepare for Chess and Logical Thinking Development

Tangram:
An ancient Chinese game consisting of 7 geometric shapes, which children use to create various figures. This game is excellent for developing:

- Creativity
- Visual-spatial awareness
- Problem-solving skills
- Logic
- Persistence and patience
- Abstract thinking
- Visual differentiation
- Self-expression
- Concentration and discipline
- Hand-eye coordination

Castle Matrix Game:
Even younger children enjoy playing with a simple castle matrix. They receive laminated versions of the missing elements of the castle, which they place in the correct spots based on shape and color. On a 3x3 grid, only the color and quantity vary.

Older children, however, draw their own matrix under more challenging conditions, sometimes on a 4x4 grid, eventually progressing to an 8x8 grid, where they must also consider directions in addition to color and quantity.

A more difficult task involves placing one piece in each row on a 4x4 matrix, with different positions in each row. Based on the shared and varying characteristics of the pieces, children must deduce the rule, create matching cards, and place them in the correct spots.

This game develops:

- Recognition and matching of shapes, colors, quantities, directions, and sizes
- Spatial orientation and perception
- Visual memory and differentiation
- Analytical and synthetic thinking
- Sorting by multiple criteria

- Pattern formation
- Patience and persistence
- Abstract thinking and mathematical constancy
- Combinatorial thinking
- Understanding of the number 8
- Familiarity with the 8x8 system, i.e., the chessboard
- Task awareness and rule-following

All these skills are essential for playing chess.

Chess Puzzle Game: This game develops:

- Logical thinking
- Visual and associative abilities
- Creativity
- Problem-solving skills
- Patience

Castle Building Game:
This is a fun drama activity where children create a "castle" using their own bodies. The teacher claps, and the children hold hands to form a castle or create any structure they choose, based on the number of claps they hear.

This game helps develop:

- Body schema and coordination
- Mathematical skills and number sense
- Logic and matching skills
- Speed and cooperation
- Social competence and rule awareness

Attention-Sharing Development Through Various Tasks: Children develop attention-sharing skills through activities like running while balancing a ball on their hand or shadow/movement games, where one child mirrors the other's actions. Traditional games like "I Lost My Handkerchief" also help develop quick reactions, attention-sharing, and strategic thinking.

Shadow Game:
One child imitates the other's first move in chess (e.g., the pawn moves

from A2 to A3). The move is always announced out loud, stating which square the piece is on. Speed is the goal. Later, when children have learned the letters and numbers, they can follow verbal instructions to move. The faster child calls out a new player, and the last one standing is the winner.

This can be prepared for with the "Rock-Paper-Scissors" game, which also develops quick reaction and situational awareness.

Physical Reaction and Focus:
Children start moving on a clap, stop on two claps, and squat on three claps. It's advisable to focus on developing gross motor skills first, then move on to fine motor activities.

For very young children (1 to 1.5 years old), reaction development is encouraged through activities like foot-powered riding with instructions to start and stop.

Learning Chess Piece Movements: After introducing each piece, children learn to place them on the board, starting with the initial setup and gradually increasing the number of pieces. They also learn the corresponding moves.

Children first practice the moves of the pieces with their bodies on a large chessboard painted on the ground. The pawn's movement is straightforward and doesn't require special preparation.

Children then learn and play with the rook's movements on the painted board, understanding that the rook moves in both rows and columns. The objective is to have the rook reach the other side as quickly as possible while avoiding obstacles. The number of obstacles can be increased, and their positions varied.
Two rooks, one white and one black, stand opposite each other and attempt to cross to the other side without colliding.
Two pairs of rooks may also move under different conditions, either by their own choice or following external instructions.

Children practice the bishop's diagonal movement ("X"), receiving similar tasks as they did with the rook.
The queen combines the movements of the rook and bishop, and children are led to understand that the more directions and squares a piece can move, the more powerful it is.

The king's movement mirrors the queen's, but it can only move one square at a time.
Finally, children practice the "knight's jump," the most complex move.

A new challenge is introduced when a child must combine the movements of two or more pieces, stepping through the board in sequence. The number of pieces gradually increases. Later, the child moves on the board following verbal instructions, either alone or in pairs.
Naturally, the pieces' costumes are made so that the children can dress up as the pieces, embodying them, and recognizing who their peers are representing.

Children first move alone on the large board, but the task becomes more difficult when an opposing piece is introduced. Here, they realize that the other side mirrors their moves, and they must pay attention.
Simultaneously, children practice the movements of the pieces on a chessboard set up in the room. They can play alone, help each other in pairs, or move as white and black pieces.
Afterward, they practice moving the pieces on smaller chessboards, drawing the moves on paper, or stepping on a paper chessboard with cut-out pieces.

First Chess Moves and Understanding Positions: Practicing/playing with one color of pieces: Different pieces are placed on the board, and another piece must navigate around its own side to reach the other side, naturally moving according to its possible moves. The goal is to raise awareness of the movements of different pieces and recognize possible positions. It's essential that the child verbalizes the situation and possible solutions.

The child then practices defending their own king on the board by placing the opposing pieces (positioning). The child must decide where to move to protect the king.

The number and complexity of positions are gradually increased based on the child's interest and receptiveness.

Building Light and Dark Knight's Castles from Cardboard:
The inhabitants of the two castles have unfortunately fallen out with each other and begin "warring." This helps the child understand that sometimes playmates can become opponents.

Introducing chess to children has many tangible (primary) benefits in their lives:

- Children develop an understanding of numbers up to 8, not just being able to count but understanding the associated quantities.
- They become familiar with basic geometric concepts, such as diagonal, row, and line, which become automatic as they learn the moves.
- By comparing the values of the pieces, they begin to grasp differences in value, laying the foundation for addition and subtraction.

Invisible Benefits:

- Establishing a foundation for lifelong learning
- Learning how to learn and developing personal strategies
- Viewing the world holistically, recognizing both sides, which leads to advanced self-evaluation skills
- Becoming more tolerant and accepting of peers (open to different ideas and opinions)
- Developing advanced logical thinking and problem-solving skills
- Understanding and applying analogies (cognitive schemas), enhancing decision-making abilities and speed (skills necessary for leadership)
- Cultivating systematic thinking
- Developing planning and creativity
- Advanced rule awareness, self-discipline, and perseverance
- Consideration and situational awareness
- High-level concentration skills and memory recall

Chess also prepares children to handle the time constraints often encountered in daily life. Therefore, it is crucial to start preparing them from an early age. Problem-solving tasks, logic-developing games, and chess are excellent tools for this purpose.

Final Words

This book journey through chess pedagogy aims to inspire, educate, and empower educators and parents alike to embrace chess as a valuable tool for enrichment. By integrating reflective elements, practical examples, and a conversational tone, the book seeks to make the educational potential of chess accessible and engaging for all.

As we reach the conclusion of this process, remember that the game of chess is much like the journey of learning itself—filled with challenges, discoveries, and opportunities for growth. May this book serve as a guide and inspiration for fostering a love of chess and learning in the hearts and minds of children everywhere.